NATIONAL DEFENSE RESEARCH INSTITUTE

FIXING LEAKS

ASSESSING THE DEPARTMENT OF DEFENSE'S APPROACH TO PREVENTING AND DETERRING UNAUTHORIZED DISCLOSURES

JAMES B. BRUCE ■ W. GEORGE JAMESON

Prepared for the Office of the Secretary of Defense
Approved for public release; distribution unlimited

The research described in this report was prepared for the Office of the Secretary of Defense (OSD). The research was conducted within the RAND National Defense Research Institute, a federally funded research and development center sponsored by OSD, the Joint Staff, the Unified Combatant Commands, the Navy, the Marine Corps, the defense agencies, and the defense Intelligence Community under Contract W74V8H-06-C-0002.

Library of Congress Cataloging-in-Publication Data is available for this publication.

ISBN: 978-0-8330-8180-3

The RAND Corporation is a nonprofit institution that helps improve policy and decisionmaking through research and analysis. RAND's publications do not necessarily reflect the opinions of its research clients and sponsors.

Support RAND—make a tax-deductible charitable contribution at www.rand.org/giving/contribute.html

RAND® is a registered trademark

Cover design by Dori Gordon Walker

© Copyright 2013 RAND Corporation

RAND OFFICES
SANTA MONICA, CA • WASHINGTON, DC
PITTSBURGH, PA • NEW ORLEANS, LA • JACKSON, MS • BOSTON, MA
DOHA, QA • CAMBRIDGE, UK • BRUSSELS, BE
www.rand.org

Preface

In 2012, the Office of the Under Secretary of Defense for Intelligence (OUSD(I)) established the Unauthorized Disclosures Program Implementation Team (UD PIT) whose mission is to *prevent and deter the unauthorized disclosures of classified information by all Department of Defense (DoD) personnel through the implementation of the UD Strategic Plan.* OUSD(I) asked RAND to help monitor and assess the potential for effectiveness of this new DoD initiative to stem unauthorized disclosures of classified information, and make recommendations as needed.

This report provides some overall observations of the RAND project team concerning the activities of the UD PIT for the period from mid-September 2012 through January 2013; then, building off those observations, the report recommends possible enhancements in the mechanisms and procedures that the UD PIT uses to accomplish its principal goals. While the study focus is limited to DoD, the recommendations may be of broader interest to the Intelligence Community (IC), since the DoD intelligence agencies and components belong to the IC and the scope of these issues is broader than DoD alone, and thus perhaps applicable to non-DoD IC elements.

This research was sponsored by OUSD(I) and conducted within the Intelligence Policy Center of the RAND National Defense Research Institute, a federally funded research and development center sponsored by the Office of the Secretary of Defense, the Joint Staff, the Unified Combatant Commands, the Navy, the Marine Corps, the defense agencies, and the defense Intelligence Community.

For more information on the RAND Intelligence Policy Center, see http://www.rand.org/nsrd/ndri/centers/ipc.html or contact the director (contact information is provided on the web page).

Contents

Figure

Summary

Introduction

Recent unauthorized disclosures (UDs) of classified information, particularly those to the public media that put sensitive operations and intelligence sources and methods at risk, have highlighted the inadequacy of extant law and policy to address the causes of and remedies to such damaging disclosures. In response to this situation, the Under Secretary of Defense for Intelligence (USD(I)) has initiated a new series of comprehensive measures, all of which are encapsulated within a Strategic Plan designed to address this heretofore intractable issue. The Plan was developed by a Department of Defense (DoD) Unauthorized Disclosures Working Group (UDWG) assembled in response to direction from the Defense Security Enterprise (DSE) Executive Committee (EXCOM) and subsequent amplifying tasking from the Under Secretary of Defense for Intelligence. Further, pursuant to the recommendations of the UDWG, OUSD(I) established an Unauthorized Disclosures Program Implementation Team (UD PIT) to oversee Strategic Plan implementation and its incremental improvement. More specifically, the UD PIT, endorsed by the Defense Security Enterprise Advisory Group (DSEAG), was established to *prevent and deter the unauthorized disclosure of classified information by all personnel through the implementation of the UD Strategic Plan.*

With a view toward enhancing its odds of success and to discover any deficiencies that, if remedied, could improve the potential effectiveness of the overall program, OUSD(I) asked the RAND Corporation to provide an outside perspective in assessing the program concept and its early implementation. Specifically, RAND was asked to monitor and assess the potential for effectiveness of the UD PIT initiative to stem UDs of classified information and to make recommendations as needed.

To meet this objective, RAND assigned two senior researchers with demonstrated expertise in UDs to support OUSD(I), the Deputy Under Secretary for Defense (DUSD) for Intelligence and Security, and the UD PIT on a part-time basis to review and assess UD Strategic Plan implementation and its early effectiveness. The researchers also engaged with appropriate personnel in DoD and in the Intelligence Community (IC) to obtain perspectives on how to improve the DoD's UD Strategic Plan content, framework, and overall implementation.

Observations on the UD PIT

The UD PIT's implementation of the UD Strategic Plan has made important and discernible progress toward its main objectives. These include clarifying reporting procedures and sanctions; achieving gains in improving awareness and training; and better integrating key supporting functions such as counterintelligence (CI), law enforcement, and legal staff. The UD PIT is exerting effective leadership in implementing a significant and comprehensive Strategic Plan that extends broadly throughout DoD. It is building a new and untried infrastructure of personnel and mechanisms to address UDs. And it is setting clearer boundaries on what is impermissible behavior in terms of the disclosure of classified information to those unauthorized to receive it.

These early successes are attributable to several factors, including that the initiative is driven by the Secretary of Defense and is top-down in nature; that the plan is well conceived and being ably executed; and that there is a broad and growing (if uneven) appreciation in the department for the seriousness of the issue at hand and the need to address it effectively.

While the early successes thus far are notable, they are also partial, fragile, and by no means permanent. Preventing and deterring the unauthorized disclosure of classified information in an

organization as large as DoD is no easy task. Even if the UD Strategic Plan were fully implemented, further efforts would be necessary to deal with the most serious part of the problem—significant classified leaks to the media, which feed voracious foreign intelligence services. To attack this tougher issue—and the one most resistant to durable solutions to the larger UD problem—the UD PIT should continue its implementation activities, but it should direct more-focused attention to establishing an end-to-end accountability process that will help transform the current "leaks-tolerant" culture that exists within DoD.

As such, addressing the problem requires overcoming both strategic and tactical obstacles. In terms of strategic obstacles, the enormity of the UD challenge is defined by three historically daunting issues that defy simple fixes: (1) media leaks have many causes but few feasible and effective solutions; (2) there is a longstanding organizational culture in DoD that treats leaking classified information to the media as nearly risk-free, which suggests to some that the behavior is acceptable; and (3) to be fully effective, remedies must address the full range of security, classification, and particularly UD-related behavior, from initial UD identification through the imposition of effective penalties for violations.

- **Many causes, hard fixes.** Of the four main factors identified in the 2005 Weapons of Mass Destruction (WMD) Commission Report as making the leaks problem nearly intractable, only one has changed: The political will to act against leakers is no longer wholly absent. The other three longstanding factors—using UDs to influence policy, the difficulty of identifying leakers, and outdated or overly narrow laws that make leaks prosecutions extremely difficult—have remained the same. Thus, any successful initiative to stem UDs must both capitalize on the recently improved political climate to reduce them and also take full account of the three remaining obstacles to controlling classified leaks. The study recommendations address these obstacles.
- **Culture of leaking.** There are many motives and reasons underlying classified leaks, including political motivations to leak to the press, the variability of classification standards across DoD

and other departments and agencies, and the everyday practical difficulty of protecting classified information. All of these nourish a culture that tolerates leaking. So few leakers ever get caught and punished, it is commonly understood that the incentives for leaking almost always outweigh the penalties. As far as the leaker is concerned, if there are no appreciable penalties and only advantages, then why stop? Solutions that will gain traction over the longer term are those that will effectively address this culture of permissiveness.

- **Establishing accountability.** A comprehensive end-to-end accountability process entails four major phases: (1) identifying and officially recording every occurrence of a UD, (2) taking or assigning "ownership" of organizational responsibility to see a case through to closure, (3) identifying who leaked the classified information, and (4) holding the leaker fully accountable for violating regulations and laws. The penalties for leaking classified information—which are too rarely applied—include a variety of administrative sanctions, civil penalties, and, in the most-serious cases, criminal prosecution.

Beyond these strategic obstacles that contribute to the very existence of UDs, there are also some important tactical obstacles the UD PIT must confront in sustaining its current accomplishments.

- **Addressing UD PIT focus issues.** Successfully addressing the unauthorized disclosures problem requires carefully calibrating the focus of the UD PIT efforts. The current focus risks being both too broad and too narrow. It is too broad in that it encompasses a wide scope of UDs—both intended and unintended, including everything from minor security infractions and other lesser breaches to deliberate leaks to the media of highly classified information. Such leaks sometimes occur in large volumes, such as WikiLeaks, or are program-jeopardizing, such as the recent disclosures about the National Security Agency collection of U.S. phone metadata and email records. The most-significant UDs require greater attention. On the other hand, the UD PIT approach is too narrow in that it focuses mostly on identification and reporting. These activities must be complemented by other, equally significant tasks, such as assigning responsibility and ownership for acting on the reported UD, seeing the action through all the needed steps to establish full accountability and appropriate sanctions for offenders, and bringing it to closure.

- **Prioritizing preventive security.** Because a key goal of the Strategic Plan is to prevent UDs, it is important to identify steps where security can act before leaks occur. The UD PIT's efforts would benefit from giving added emphasis to a review of DoD measures that will ensure clarity and effective implementation of existing requirements, as well as determining where new measures could improve the vetting process. Specifically, the following three areas require attention: existing standards for security clearances, rules to limit unsupervised access by even security-cleared personnel to the most-sensitive information, and timely electronic monitoring capabilities that can identify insider threats and other attempts to obtain unauthorized access.

- **Clarifying the language and guidance in addressing UDs.** The language and guidance addressing UDs are often unclear and inconsistent, which argues for the UD PIT taking steps to ensure that DoD directives, manuals, and other issuances—and guidance from senior officials—are clear and consistent.

- **Creating metrics.** While much attention is given to numbers of UDs, little has been paid to those metrics that focus on results or that can help with understanding what will deter and prevent UDs. DoD's metrics effort is still nascent. Until the UD PIT is able to deliver a richer level of detail, there will be few actionable insights that reach beyond identifying and tracking UDs. Similarly, there is a need to establish an analytic focus that addresses the causes of leaks, their consequences, and how to prevent them.

- **Addressing CI and security issues.** The UD PIT must resolve sensitivity issues, ambiguities, and even resistance where CI interests arise regarding the obligation of all DoD elements, including CI, to formally report UDs to the Director of Security Policy and Oversight, OUSD(I), in a timely manner. Additionally, a major security issue is the adequacy of vetting of U.S. government and contractor personnel for access to classified and sensitive information, as well as the adequacy of day-to-day security measures to detect insider threats and oversight of their implementation. For example, both Edward Snowden and Bradley Manning are responsible for significant UDs that might have been prevented; both had evinced behavioral issues that, in retrospect, should have raised questions about their suitability for access to classified information.

- **Making UD process improvements:** Organizational and management issues related to the authority and functioning of the UD PIT require clarification and possible changes to improve direction and component responsiveness.
- **Having more outreach and integration:** The UD effort has made considerable headway, and the OUSD(I) Security Policy and Oversight Directorate and, increasingly, UD PIT membership have been suitably engaged, but greater UD PIT outreach and attention to other major stakeholders with equities in addressing the UD problem will leverage gains and effectiveness.

Recommendations

The 22 recommendations offered in this report are keyed on sustaining the successes that the UD PIT has already achieved. They also seek to enhance and focus UD PIT efforts to address any uncompleted actions, shortfalls, and other areas of the DoD UD Strategic Plan that warrant priority attention. They span UD PIT management, culture and accountability, policy and new initiatives, and studies and outreach.

UD PIT Management

1. **Hold your ground.** Revalidate the UD Strategic Plan and the importance of the UD PIT. Maintain and consolidate the gains already established.

2. **Expand your ground.** Grow the UD initiative through a re-calibrated and even more ambitious agenda, as well as through greater DoD-wide senior-level oversight and direction.

3. **Sustain the top-down approach.** With the recent transition in Defense Secretaries, ensure that the top-level priority and support assigned to the UD initiative by the previous Secretary is reinforced and sustained by the new leadership.

4. **Enhance UD PIT authority.** Empower UD PIT members within their components and establish a Senior Executive Service (SES)–level UD steering group, possibly a subgroup of the DSE EXCOM, to which the PIT should regularly report.

5. **Focus on the significant UDs.** With prioritization guidance worked out by the Program Management Office (PMO), direct the PIT's focus to the most-serious classified disclosures to the media.

6. **Establish metrics to track results.** After counting the numbers of UDs, a more granular system of categorizing them and tracking end-to-end results is needed to better evaluate the performance of the PIT and PMO in accomplishing their mission.

Culture and Accountability

7. **Connect culture change with UD results.** Establishing full UD accountability by identifying leakers and applying sanctions will promote the realization that leakers will be caught and punished.

8. **Ensure end-to-end accountability for results.** The PIT should ensure that full ownership of every serious UD is assumed or assigned, that accountability is established as offenders are identified and adjudicated, and that appropriate sanctions are implemented before any serious case is brought to closure.

9. **Energize the three-track system.** Clarify policies, directives, and guidance to help managers understand their authorities and responsibilities to ensure that accountability is established as identified offenders are punished for violations.

10. **Facilitate compliance through a reasonable approach.** An effective system will facilitate, not inhibit, compliance; sanctions must be timely, visible, meaningful, and fair.

11. **Prioritize and deliver quality UD training and education.** A workforce that is more knowledgeable and alert to UDs will get on board, improve compliance, and support culture change.

Policy and New Initiatives

12. **Align UD language with PIT goals.** Ensure language clarity and consistency in all relevant DoD documents, directives, manuals, and official issuances—and along the full range of departmental authorities.

13. **Resolve classification and sensitivity barriers.** Ensure that, regardless of sensitivity, UDs involving CI, the Inspector General (IG), law enforcement, Sensitive Compartmented Information (SCI), Special Access Program (SAP), and Alternative Compensatory Control Measures (ACCM) are reported to the Security Policy and Oversight Directorate in a timely manner.

14. **Review Security Vetting for Classified Access.** The UD PIT should elevate the importance of security vetting in its Strategic Plan and help lead an effort to review and reform such DoD security measures that should include a reliable and predictive evaluation of security trustworthiness.

15. **Leverage technology.** Review available technologies and develop or adapt new technologies that will enhance the implementation of the Strategic Plan and related initiatives for training, analytic, and investigatory purposes, as well as the protection of information and systems.

16. **Lay the foundation for comprehensive leaks legislation.** Identify promising attributes of more-effective laws addressing UDs, brief the Armed Services and Intelligence Committees on the Strategic Plan, and build support among those committees, the White House, and others for submitting draft leaks legislation.

Studies and Outreach

17. **Conduct a comprehensive study of UDs.** Such a study should assess causes, consequences, and correctives that will help in understanding UDs, enhancing prioritization efforts, and sustaining the effectiveness of the UD program over the long haul.

18. **Study ways to improve the identification of leakers (Step 3 of the end-to-end accountability process discussed in Chapter Two).** Review available analytic, technological, collaborative, and other investigatory tools and develop new ones to identify leakers.

19. **Study ways to improve the implementation of sanctions when leakers are identified (Step 4 of the end-to-end accountability process discussed in Chapter Two).** Review the three-track sanctions options—administrative, civil, and criminal—for maximum applicability.

20. **Expand outreach.** The UD PIT should take advantage of the expertise and lessons learned from the numerous organizations outside of USD(I) that have interests and equities in supporting the PIT UD goals.

21. **Seek closer alignment with the ODNI and other IC approaches to UDs.** Ensure that separate IC and DoD action tracks are appropriately synchronized with each other.

22. **Engage the Inspectors General.** The role of the IG in supporting the top-down initiative should be defined, with particular emphasis on identifying systemic problems in the implementation of the Strategic Plan and other UD-related mechanisms, practices, and shortcomings, as well as investigations into which IG authorities may be valuable in crossing organizational lines.

Acknowledgments

This study benefited greatly from the openness, accessibility, and ready assistance of the leadership of the UD PIT and other team members who made every effort to provide requested information and helpful insights in support of this effort. In consultations outside of DoD, senior experts from CIA's Office of Security and the National Counterintelligence Executive offered especially valuable perspectives during the research. Additionally, thorough and constructive critiques of an earlier draft provided by RAND staff Robert Murrett, Michael McNerney, and Paul Steinberg have much enhanced the quality and clarity of this report.

Abbreviations

CI	counterintelligence
CMIS	Corporate Management Information System
DoD	Department of Defense
DoJ	Department of Justice
DSE	Defense Security Enterprise
EXCOM	executive committee
IC	Intelligence Community
IG	Inspector General
ISOO	Information Security Oversight Office
NSC	National Security Council
ODNI	Office of the Director of National Intelligence
OGC	Office of the General Counsel
OUSD(I)	Office of the Under Secretary of Defense for Intelligence
PMO	Program Management Office
SCI	Sensitive Compartmented Information
SES	Senior Executive Service
SIR	Security Incident Report
UD	unauthorized disclosure
UD PIT	Unauthorized Disclosures Program Implementation Team
UDWG	Unauthorized Disclosures Working Group
USD(I)	Under Secretary of Defense for Intelligence
WMD	weapons of mass destruction

CHAPTER ONE

Introduction

As a newspaper, *The Post* thrives on revelatory journalism and often benefits from leaks, sometimes inspired by dissent and other times by spin.

—Washington Post Editorial Board[1]

I am sorry for the unintended consequences of my actions. When I made these decisions, I believed I was going to help people, not hurt people.

—Pfc. Bradley Manning[2]

Background

Recent unauthorized disclosures of classified information, particularly those to the public media that put sensitive operations and intelligence sources and methods at risk, have highlighted the inadequacy of extant law and policy to address the causes of, and remedies to, such damaging unauthorized disclosures (UDs). In response to this situation, the Office of the Under Secretary of Defense for Intelligence (OUSD(I))

---

[1]   Washington Post Editorial Board, "Not Every Leak Is Tantamount to Treason," *Washington Post*, August 1, 2013.

[2]   Courtney Kube, Matthew DeLuca, and Erin McClam, "'I'm Sorry That I Hurt the United States': Bradley Manning Apologizes in Court," NBCNews.com website, August 14, 2013.

initiated a new series of comprehensive measures, all of which are encapsulated within a Strategic Plan that is designed to address this heretofore intractable issue across all components of the Department of Defense (DoD). This Strategic Plan was developed by the DoD Unauthorized Disclosures Working Group (UDWG). The group was assembled from April through May 18, 2012 in response to direction from the Defense Security Enterprise (DSE) Executive Committee (EXCOM) and follow-on amplifying tasking from the Under Secretary of Defense for Intelligence (USD(I)).[3] Emphasizing the priority of this initiative, then–Secretary of Defense Leon Panetta issued a memorandum establishing a "top-down" approach to addressing UDs.[4]

Further, OUSD(I) established an Unauthorized Disclosures Program Implementation Team (UD PIT) to oversee Strategic Plan implementation and its incremental improvement. More specifically, the group, endorsed by the Defense Security Enterprise Advisory Group (DSEAG), was established to *prevent and deter the unauthorized disclosure of classified information by all personnel through the implementation of the UD Strategic Plan*. Its mandate to achieve that mission is to:

- implement the UDWG Strategic Plan to prevent unintentional unauthorized disclosures and deter intentional ones (empowered to craft enterprise change)
- comprehensively improve security awareness, education, and training
- clarify administrative processes, procedures, and sanctions in policy
- improve information technology enablement of these processes and procedures

---

[3]   Under Secretary of Defense for Intelligence, "Improving Policy and Procedures for Unauthorized Disclosures Reporting," memorandum, June 19, 2012, and "Clarification of Policy for Management of Unauthorized Disclosures," memorandum, October 2, 2012.

[4]   U.S. Secretary of Defense, "Deterring and Preventing Unauthorized Disclosures of Classified Information," memorandum, October 18, 2012.

- improve integration, including aligning key supporting functions and organizations (counterintelligence [CI], law enforcement, information assurance), legal staff, and external partners.[5]

The UD PIT stakeholders include the DoD Components, Office of the Director of National Intelligence (ODNI) Staff Elements, Intelligence Community (IC) Elements and the employees of each.

Because the UD problem has been so resistant to correctives in the past, much will depend on how rigorously the Strategic Plan is implemented by the UD PIT and DoD Components.

Objective and Approach

With a view toward enhancing its odds of success and to discover any deficiencies that, if remedied, could improve the potential effectiveness of the overall program, OUSD(I) asked the RAND Corporation to provide an outside perspective in assessing the program concept and its early implementation. Specifically, RAND was asked to monitor and assess the potential for effectiveness of the UD PIT initiative to stem UDs of classified information, and to make recommendations as needed.

To meet this objective, RAND assigned two senior researchers with demonstrated expertise in UDs to support the OUSD(I), the Deputy Under Secretary for Defense (DUSD) for Intelligence & Security, and the UD PIT on a part-time basis to review and assess the UD Strategic Plan's implementation and effectiveness. The researchers participated in every weekly UD PIT meeting that took place during the four-month period of the study (mid-September 2012 through January 2013) either in person and jointly or, on rare occasions, singly or remotely by conference call. RAND provided periodic written inputs to the UD PIT process through numerous emails, substantive memos, and critiques and commentary on many UD PIT-generated documents and presentation slides.

---

[5]   The source for this was material regularly included in UD PIT meeting agendas.

Defining Unauthorized Disclosures ("Leaks") and Security Violations

Unauthorized Disclosure (UD) is defined as "communication or physical transfer of classified or controlled unclassified information to an unauthorized recipient."

Applicability of UD security policies, directives, authorities, and responsibilities extends to the "Office of the Secretary of Defense, the Military Departments, the Chairman of the Joint Chiefs of Staff, the Combatant Commands, the office of the Inspector General of the Department of Defense, the Defense Agencies, the DoD Field Activities, and all other organizational entities of the Department of Defense (hereinafter referred to collectively as the "DoD Components")."

Security incidents related to UDs include:

- Infractions: failure to comply with requirements that do not result in the loss, suspected compromise, or compromise of classified information.
- Violations: security incidents that indicate knowing, willful, and negligent action that does or could result in loss or compromise.
- Compromise: security violation in which there is an unauthorized disclosure of classified information (where the recipient does not have a valid clearance, authorized access, or need to know).
- Loss occurs when classified information cannot be physically located or accounted for.

SOURCE: DoD, *DoD Information Security Program: Protection of Classified Information, Glossary*, Manual 5200.01-Volume 3, Enclosure 6, February 24, 2012a (as amended).

Scope

The scope of this effort was defined by the four-month, part-time engagement of the researchers acting in an advisory and consulting capacity, the quick-turnaround nature of the observations and critiques, a qualitative versus quantitative approach, and no in-depth research of issues that require it. (Indeed, several recommendations identify areas where substantial research is needed.) Additionally, the term *unauthorized disclosure* spans a far broader range of activity than the scope of this report (see page 4). UDs can be intentional or unintentional; involve espionage or carelessness, acts of policy advocates, whistleblowers, or malcontents; or even press leaks inspired by senior leaders. As agreed upon early in the project definition, the particular focus of this report is on significant leaks of classified information deliberately provided to the media that are damaging to DoD.

Organization of the Document

In Chapter Two, we provide some overall observations and impressions about the activities of the UD PIT for the period from mid-September 2012 through January 2013. Building off those observations and impressions, in Chapter Three we provide recommendations about possible enhancements in the mechanisms and procedures that the UD PIT uses to accomplish its principal goals.

The report also contains two appendixes: Appendix A presents a summary of a discussion with UD PIT leadership about determining thresholds for taking legal actions against a leaker of classified information, while Appendix B presents responses to four specific questions posed by OUSD(I) during the project, including leaking by seniors, overclassification and proving damage, freedom-of-press issues, and intrusive measures to monitor employee conduct.

CHAPTER TWO

Observations on UD PIT Effectiveness

As noted previously, the research approach entailed the authors' participation in every weekly UD PIT meeting that took place during the four-month period of the study, separate consultations or informational conversations with a number of relevant individuals or subject-matter experts involved with UDs, and a document review and related background research about UDs. Based on these activities, the authors' observations and impressions about the UD PIT process are offered here, with recommendations for improvement in the next chapter.

The bottom-line findings are that *the UD PIT has done a solid job to date implementing a well-conceived and ambitious strategic plan. It has made discernible progress toward its goals, but we also identified some continuing needs that must be met to ensure the progress is sustained.*

The UD PIT Has Made Discernible Progress to Date

The scope of DoD-wide engagement in the UD initiative is notable. Less than a year ago, this major initiative did not even exist, and even before the Strategic Plan was formally approved, UD PIT took early actions for its implementation. The cumulative effect is incremental, and progress is discernible. Specifically, the UD PIT's efforts have led to important progress in each of the three broad focus areas identified in the Strategic Plan: (1) clarification of processes, procedures, and sanctions; (2) the need to improve awareness, education, and training; and (3) the need for better integration and alignment of key supporting functions and disciplines (such as CI, law enforcement, information assurance, legal staff, and external partners).

More specifically, the accomplishments include the following:

- **Significant initiative.** The UD PIT's implementation of the well-designed Strategic Plan to stem UDs is ambitious and potentially sustainable for the long term.
- **Comprehensive approach.** The Strategic Plan spans nearly all of the key aspects of a DoD-wide approach to addressing what has been a serious, long-standing, and nearly intractable issue.
- **Broad reach.** The Strategic Plan has engaged a significant number of DoD personnel, most of whom seem dedicated to the task, share the goals of the UD PIT, and devote time and energy to supporting the implementation of the plan in their respective components.
- **Building UD infrastructure.** This wide-ranging activity to design and implement a comprehensive plan has created an infrastructure of processes and designated personnel with a shared purpose, direction, and responsibility to reduce UDs and mitigate the harm they cause.
- **Effective leadership.** The daunting task is made easier and more manageable by the UD PIT leadership's carefully planned direction, focus on bite-size pieces, and reasonable tasking. It operates with a light touch, avoids heavy-handed directives, and sets achievable goals with firm but reachable deadlines, allowing adequate time to accomplish the action. If more time is needed, it is granted where appropriate.
- **Setting boundaries.** The UD PIT has begun to clarify to senior department officials that leaking is impermissible through the following important initiatives:
  - providing responsibility and awareness briefings for senior officials that explain DoD's policy that UDs are unacceptable and illegal, and that violations may result in penalties
  - providing memos for incoming and outgoing Senior Executive Service (SES)–level political appointees, removing any ambiguity about the restrictions on providing classified information

to unauthorized personnel, especially those in the media, while in office and after leaving office
- updating and improving a trifold informational fact sheet that presents FAQs and answers and clearly and unambiguously communicates DoD policy on prepublication review requirements.
- **Reporting procedures.** A major set of actions in the Strategic Plan establishes a DoD-wide mechanism for reporting and tracking UDs. Transitioning from using the Security Incident Report (SIR) system to the Corporate Management Information System (CMIS), this requirement prioritizes every UD as a reportable security breach and seeks the full engagement of every DoD security component in identifying, reporting, and tracking UDs through a process that will prompt follow-up actions of every case until formal closure. A flow chart being developed to standardize and track leak actions throughout DoD represents a major step in clarifying responsibilities and processes.

The successes that the UD PIT has experienced thus far are attributable to several factors:

- **The initiative is driven from the top down.** With the direction of the Secretary of Defense and the support of the most-senior leadership in DoD, it is bureaucratically hard to resist.
- **The Strategic Plan is well conceived and is being ably executed.** The UD PIT leadership has a sound understanding of the issue and is fully committed to the goals of the Strategic Plan and to carrying out the elements of its implementation using a nonthreatening, collegial approach.
- **In some of the key components of DoD, there seems to be broad appreciation for the seriousness of the issue, the complexity of the task, and the need to address it.**

Despite these favorable factors, lasting success is by no means assured. The major DoD management challenge to achieve success against UDs over the long haul must sustain and institutionalize the fledgling UD-mitigation infrastructure and its notable accomplishments. And it must expand the infrastructure's scope and effectiveness against the pattern of leaks, especially the most-damaging ones. The nature and scale of the obstacles in the path to durable success are deeply rooted and broad-based.

Tackling a Historically Intractable Problem

Although notable, the early successes in the UD initiative thus far are also partial, fragile, and by no means permanent. Preventing and deterring the unauthorized disclosure of classified information in such a large organization that has grappled with the problem and its complexities and sensitivities for so long is no easy task. The Strategic Plan includes security and other measures to prevent and deter both unintentional and intentional UDs. All these measures set forth in the Plan are important and, if implemented fully, will go a long way toward deterring and preventing UDs.

However, while these tasks are incremental steps that can reduce some UDs, more must be done to deal with the most serious part of the problem—significant classified leaks to the media and the public. To tackle that issue, which undermines the effectiveness of the Strategic Plan's implementation and results in significant harm to national security interests, the UD PIT should direct more-focused attention on establishing an end-to-end accountability process that will help transform the current "leaks-tolerant" culture within DoD and give added "oomph" to the specific measures mandated by the Strategic Plan.

It is important to acknowledge that DoD's approach to the management of UDs is a full-spectrum program addressing not only leaks to the media, but other security violations involving the unauthorized disclosure of classified information. Still, the bulk of serious UDs in DoD involve disclosure to the media of classified military operations and intelligence sources and methods, and these UDs accordingly serve as the emphasis of this report.

The UD initiative entails substantial obstacles that must be understood and addressed both *strategically* and *tactically* if the initiative is to succeed fully over the long haul. We discuss both of those obstacles below.

Strategic Obstacles to Overcome

Strategic obstacles to full UD PIT success include the following:

- UDs have many causes but few feasible and effective solutions.
- A long-standing organizational culture in many U.S. government organizations, including DoD, seems willing to accept that leaking classified information to the media is risk-free and, accordingly, acceptable.
- To be effective, the remedies need to address the full range of UD behavior, from initial identification through effective penalties for violations.

Many Causes, Hard Fixes

All agree that the UD problem has multiple causes and has been resistant to solutions. As documented in its 2005 report, the Presidential Commission on the Intelligence Capabilities Regarding Weapons of Mass Destruction (WMD) found that the causes of leaks are multiple, the effects serious, and the remedies elusive. The Commission explained:

> The scope of damage done to our collection capabilities from media disclosures of classified information is well documented. Hundreds of serious press leaks have significantly impaired U.S. capabilities against our hardest targets. [Leaks] have collectively cost the American people hundreds of millions of dollars, and have done grave harm to national security.

According to past government studies, the long-standing inability of the U.S. government to control press leaks results from a combination of factors—the use of unauthorized disclosures as a vehicle to influence policy, the lack of political will to deal firmly and consistently with government leakers in both the executive and legislative branches, the difficulty of prosecuting cases under existing statutes, and the challenge of identifying the leaker. The government's impotence in dealing effectively with this problem was well characterized by then-Deputy Assistant Attorney General Richard K. Willard, in 1982:

In summary, past experience with leaks investigations has been largely unsuccessful and uniformly frustrating for all concerned. . . . The whole system has been so ineffectual as to perpetuate the notion that the Government can do nothing to stop the leaks.

The Commission recognizes the enormous difficulty of this seemingly intractable problem and has considered a broad range of potential solutions. We conclude that the long-standing defeatism that has paralyzed action on this topic is understandable but unwarranted. Leaks cannot be stopped, but they can be reduced. And those responsible for the most damaging leaks can be held accountable if they can be identified and if the government is willing to prosecute them.[1]

Importantly, of the four main factors identified by the commission as hindering the ability to control the leaking of classified information, only one has changed since the Commission study was published in 2005: *The political will to act against leakers is no longer wholly absent.*[2] The other three factors—using UDs to influence policy, the difficulty of identifying leakers, and outdated or overly narrow laws

---

[1]   Commission on the Intelligence Capabilities of the United States Regarding Weapons of Mass Destruction, *Report to the President of the United States* [Silberman-Robb WMD Commission Report], Washington, D.C.: U.S. Government Printing Office, 2005, pp. 381–382, italics added; citing the National Counterintelligence Policy Board, *Report to the NSC* [National Security Council] *on Unauthorized Media Leak Disclosures*, March 1996, pp. C2–C4. The Willard quotation is cited from *Report of the Interdepartmental Group on Unauthorized Disclosures of Classified Information*, March 31, 1982. The WMD Commission was established to explain the intelligence failure in which WMD programs thought to exist in Iraq were no longer there at the time of the National Intelligence Estimate that described them in detail as if they were.

[2]   This is evidenced by the number of cases the current Department of Justice (DoJ) has brought against leakers after a 28-year hiatus during which previous administrations did not bring a single case to trial, the heightened congressional interest in draft legislation to better control leaks, and corresponding efforts within the IC at the ODNI level and in sev-

that make leaks prosecutions extremely difficult—have remained constant. Thus, to be successful, any initiative to stem UDs must fully capitalize on the recently improved political climate to reduce UDs, while also taking full account of the other main obstacles to controlling classified leaks. The recommendations in Chapter Three include actions beyond the scope of the present UD PIT Strategic Plan that are mindful of the motivations for leaking, identifying leakers, and the need for a comprehensive sanctions scheme for dealing more effectively with leaks of classified information.[3]

Culture of Leaking

Despite the myriad laws, regulations, and nondisclosure agreements that strictly prohibit disclosing classified information to persons not authorized to receive it, the scope and seriousness of leaks over the years have shown the ineffectiveness of the rules designed to protect classified information and keep it out of the media and the public domain. The significant damage that classified leaks cause to U.S. intelligence collection capabilities—and thus to analysis and intelligence support to policymakers and warfighters—is far better documented in classified studies than in the public domain.[4] Yet leaks continue apace. Indeed, in DoD, as in other government organizations that handle classified information and whose personnel regularly interact—often anonymously—with the media on major policy issues, leaking has long been a commonplace activity.

---

eral major agencies to tighten internal controls over leaking, including DoD's top-down UD initiative.

[3] Infirmities in the legal framework for dealing with leaks are thoroughly examined in Eric E. Ballou and Kyle E. McSlarrow, "Plugging the Leak: A Case for Legislative Resolution of the Conflict between Demands of Secrecy and the Need for an Open Government," *Virginia Law Review*, June 1985, pp. 801–868.

[4] Documentation of the damage that leaks cause to intelligence capabilities is available in classified government studies. A summary of these findings and references was provided to the sponsor separately through secure channels. A more limited but publicly available study addressing damage is James B. Bruce, "How Leaks of Classified Intelligence Help U.S. Adversaries: Implications for Laws and Secrecy," in Roger Z. George and Robert D. Kline, eds., *Intelligence and the National Security Strategist: Enduring Issues and Challenges*, Washington, D.C.: National Defense University Press, 2004, pp. 399–414.

Motivations for leaking vary widely, including the political impetus to support or oppose policy, ego gratification, cultivating goodwill with the media, whistleblowing, and self-interest for personal or professional advantage. Whatever the motive, the activity is widespread. A Harvard study found that a remarkable 42 percent of former federal officials in policy positions who responded to its survey had disclosed classified information to the media. While the cultural attributes of leaking have not been studied directly, knowledgeable observers agree that *leaking to the press is indeed a cultural attribute of many U.S. government organizations, including DoD.*[5]

The leaking culture is a conflicted one, demonstrating difficulty balancing secrecy with the principles of openness important to ensuring that the citizenry is informed about the operations of government and the accountability of government itself. A series of factors pose challenges for those who seek to protect information: constitutionally protected freedom of the press, anonymous sources, whistleblower protections, poor enforcement, and the practical difficulties of disseminating classified information securely, particularly in an Internet environment. At the same time, it is ironic that, in a department with a culture that requires military discipline to accomplish its missions, there is such an apparent lack of discipline about keeping classified information out of the press. This is partly because classified leaks are used to support or oppose political or policy objectives; partly because classification standards are not consistently understood or applied across DoD components and other departments and agencies (discussed in Appendix B); and partly because the protection of classified information is sometimes inconvenient, often seen as standing in the way of the efficient conduct of business. Finally, if infrequently, occasional press leaks are reportedly approved by senior officials. While this may be a rare occurrence, it further confounds understanding among DoD

---

[5]   The relevant literature on leaks supports this observation. See Gary Ross, *Who Watches the Watchmen: The Conflict Between National Security and Freedom of the Press*, Washington, D.C.: National Intelligence Press, 2011. Ross cites data from the Harvard study and from Elie Abel, *Leaking: Who Does It? Who Benefits at What Cost?* New York: Priority Press Publications, 1987. See also Gabriel Schoenfeld, *Necessary Secrets: National Security, the Media, and the Rule of Law*, New York: W.W. Norton, 2010; and the Willard Report.

personnel about what is acceptable and what is not because it is done opaquely. This practice tends to lend legitimacy to leaking.

Regardless of rationale, so few leakers ever get caught and punished that it is commonly understood that the incentives to leak almost always outweigh the penalties. Despite the UD PIT's notable accomplishments in implementing the Strategic Plan thus far, perhaps the most difficult issue associated with leaks remains unaddressed: If there are only advantages and no appreciable penalties for leaking, then why stop? This cycle of permissibility is continuous and self-reinforcing.[6]

Changing this culture of permissiveness may be the most daunting challenge to designing and implementing durable correctives to UD behavior. Thus, the solutions that will gain traction over the longer term are those that effectively address this culture of permissiveness that provides more incentives than disincentives to leak classified information. The enormous frustration of government impotence in dealing with this problem, identified nearly 30 years ago in the findings of the Willard Report,[7] has only worsened, leading to resignation and inaction because of the extreme difficulty of identifying government leakers. Worse, even if the leaker's identity can be determined, carrying out punishment is improbably burdensome. Terminating employment or even suspending clearances can be a long and painful bureaucratic process. Prosecuting cases imposes an extremely high legal standard under espionage statutes and can also risk additional release of classified information in court proceedings. Even some senior officials and military commanders do not always view UD-generated actions as important or "mission" activities, despite the harm that disclosures can cause to military operations and preparedness and to intelligence sources and methods.

---

[6] See James B. Bruce, "Laws and Leaks of Classified Intelligence: The Consequences of Permissive Neglect," *Studies in Intelligence*, Vol. 47, No. 1, March, 2003, pp. 39–49; Bruce, 2004; and W. George Jameson, "Safeguarding National Security Information: Dealing with Unauthorized Disclosures of Classified Information," *Conference Reports: "National Security, Law in a Changed World: The Twelfth Annual Review of the Field,"* American Bar Association, *National Security Law Report*, Vol. 25, No. 1, May 2003.

[7] *Report of the Interdepartmental Group on Unauthorized Disclosures of Classified Information* [Willard Report], March 31, 1982.

Because much of the leaking of classified information is the result of a culture of acceptance and permissibility, changing that culture to one that will prevent and deter UDs requires both declaratory policy and demonstrable actions that result in real consequences for violating security and nondisclosure rules, breaching trust relationships, and breaking the law.

Training and awareness are vital components in culture formation. But current training in UD prevention is woefully inadequate. The UD PIT has already taken important steps under the Strategic Plan to initiate, upgrade, and implement training and awareness activities that highlight the damage caused by UDs and the importance of personal responsibility in protecting classified information. Nevertheless, as described below, much more effort is needed to reinforce this vital message and help change the current culture.

Establishing Accountability: An End-to-End Approach

For all the gains of the UD PIT Strategic Plan, its implementation challenges certainly highlight the difficulties of getting beyond the first steps—measures that deal with tightening security and identifying and reporting a UD—to the harder, follow-up measures of reinforcement and sanctioning offenders for conduct that is illegal or, at a minimum, a violation of nondisclosure agreements and the public trust.

As seen in Figure 2.1, a comprehensive, end-to-end accountability process entails four major phases, each with its own challenges:

1. *Identifying and Reporting.* UDs must be identified and officially recorded. This basic step, without which nothing else can happen, is a major focus of the Strategic Plan. When the reporting vehicle transitions from SIR to CMIS, it will be further improved.

2. *Taking Ownership.* Unless a senior official in an organization is willing to claim responsibility for pursuing a UD in his or her element or component—thereby assuming organizational

Figure 2.1
End-to-End Accountability Process

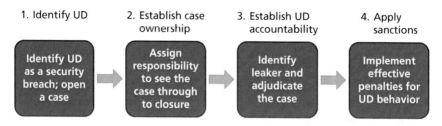

RAND *RR409-2.1*

responsibility to see the case through to closure—no additional action beyond the reporting of a UD event is likely to occur.[8]

3. *Establishing Accountability.* Leakers cannot be held accountable for their violations unless they can be identified. Even if identified, accused leakers must then undergo some kind of adjudication process that will make a determination of innocence or guilt. If found guilty, offenders must feel the full weight of sanctions commensurate with the seriousness of the breach.

4. *Applying Sanctions.* Penalties for leaking classified information can occur on any of three tracks, or some combination of them, each with an increasing degree of severity:

   ○ **administrative sanctions**, e.g., reprimand, loss of pay, loss of clearances, reassignment, demotion, or termination of employment

   ○ **civil penalties**, such as the loss of royalties in the case of a book publication that averted official review and/or disclosed classified information[9]

---

[8] Recently, a two-star Combatant Commander Chief of Staff formally sought to excuse his entire command from the responsibility of even conducting requested classification and security reviews of manuscripts and publications, which he complained was resource-intensive and a distraction from the command's mission.

[9] See *Snepp v. United States*, 444 U.S. 507, U.S. Supreme Court, February 19, 1980; and, more recently, *United States v. Ishmael Jones*, U.S. District Court for the Eastern District of Virginia, April 18, 2012.

- **criminal prosecution**, while rare, is well-established in the 1985 *Morison* case, and several new ones begun during the Obama administration.[10]

Fully implementing and providing consistent departmental guidance for this three-track system for sanctioning offenders will establish the seriousness of this effort and help institutionalize its longer-term effectiveness. Uncompromising accountability, when it can be established, is essential to dealing with intentional UDs—that is, the unauthorized disclosure of classified information to the media and the public.

Such disclosures are different, we note, from the "authorized leaks," wherein government officials either disclose classified information to the media and the public, or direct their subordinates to do so. To the extent that such disclosures flout applicable authorities for the classification, declassification, and dissemination of classified information—whether out of convenience, time constraints, perceived necessity, or confusion over obligations—the disclosure of such "authorized" leaked information will undermine the end-to-end accountability system that depends on employee assurance that the "rules apply to everyone."[11]

The current statutory framework also complicates accountability. The laws for prosecuting leakers of classified information consist of a variety of statutes that do not provide an effective, comprehensive legislative approach; in fact, such statutes are typically a barrier to enforce-

---

[10] *United States v. Morison*, 844 F.2d 1057, United States Court of Appeals for the 4th Circuit, April 1, 1988, a prosecution for disclosing classified information to the media; and *United States v. John C. Kiriakou*, U.S. District Court for the Eastern District of Virginia, January 23, 2013, for revealing the covert identity of CIA employees.

[11] We note that Congress, to address such "authorized leaks," recently enacted requirements for the timely notification to Congress of the "authorized disclosure" of intelligence to the press or the public if that intelligence is classified or if it has been declassified for the purpose of the disclosure. (Public Law 112–277, Intelligence Authorization Act for Fiscal Year 2013, Section 504, January 14, 2013.) Although some disclosures could satisfy the requirement that there is a "need to know" to further the government's business, the disclosure of classified information also must comply with applicable requirements that recipients be "trustworthy" (i.e., possess security clearances) and sign a secrecy nondisclosure agreement.

ment.[12] Except perhaps for two narrowly drawn statutes addressing the disclosure of identities of covert human agents and communications intelligence, the laws generally cited as providing authority to prosecute leakers are those dealing with theft of government property and the 1917 espionage statute. Both present significant enforcement hurdles. Only rarely can a case meet the espionage standard required for prosecution. The focus of those laws on damage to national defense is not seen as synonymous with damage to national security, and intent to cause damage is extremely difficult to prove. Further, a leaker is rarely caught in possession of the stolen goods. Additionally, while damage from UDs can be equivalent to or even worse than spying because UDs afford broader availability of sensitive classified information to all the foreign intelligence services that read the U.S. press, those who leak secrets to the public are not often seen in the same light as spies who clandestinely disclose secrets to foreign espionage services one at a time. Rather, leakers often claim whistleblower or free-speech motivations. Thresholds for legal action are discussed in Appendix A.

Only the vigorous development and application of an end-to-end approach can address the significant challenge of changing a culture of permissiveness that tolerates the leaking of classified information. While the present Strategic Plan is particularly strong on the reporting function, the other three phases in this end-to-end accountability process are underemphasized or missing. Technology can help. As the technological improvements in shifting from SIR to CMIS will improve the reporting function, so too can better technologies improve performance in the other accountability steps, especially Step 3 in leaker identification. Technology-aided or not, until better UD accountability is established and sanctions applied, hopes for a reduction in serious UDs will almost certainly be disappointed.

The recommendations in Chapter Three aim to address these strategic factors that contribute to UDs; namely, that serious leaks have many causes and no easy fixes, and that cultural attributes in DoD (and other organizations) must be changed to make any appreciable

---

[12] For elaboration, see studies by Ballou and McSlarrow, 1985; Bruce, 2004; and Jameson, 2003.

headway in preventing and deterring leaks. Finally, to change organizational cultures, nothing less than a full end-to-end approach to accountability that results in meaningful sanctions is required. Thus, some of these recommendations go well beyond the scope of the present Strategic Plan because fully accomplishing the UD PIT goals of preventing and deterring UDs will require such actions.

Tactical Obstacles to Overcome

Beyond the strategic obstacles that contribute to the difficulty of preventing and deterring UDs, there are also some important tactical obstacles the UD PIT must confront to sustain and expand its current accomplishments.

UD PIT Efforts Have Focus Issues

Successfully addressing the leaks problem requires carefully calibrating the focus of the UD PIT efforts. This focus currently risks being both too broad and too narrow. On the one hand, UDs encompass a wide scope of activities, including those that are intended as well as unintended. UDs include everything from minor security violations and other lesser breaches to deliberate leaks of highly classified information to the media. More-serious UDs are notable for their scale (e.g., the massive WikiLeaks disclosures) and their potential damage to military capabilities and operations and to sensitive sources and methods (e.g., publication of *No Easy Day*, a book revealing classified and closely-guarded details of the Osama bin Laden take-down operation). While all security incidents do indeed require a regularized reporting and tracking mechanism, a more concerted and timely focus on the most-serious security breaches, particularly damaging media leaks, will help identify where to direct scarce resources to best address priority UDs. The new CMIS reporting requirements should allow for categorizing UDs by relative importance.

But on the other hand, this necessary early focus on UD identification and reporting will be too narrow in the long run. It must be complemented by other equally significant tasks, such as taking responsibility and ownership for acting on the reported UD, seeing the action through all the needed steps (i.e., those identified in a UD PIT flow chart being designed to standardize and track leak actions) to establish full accountability and appropriate sanctions for offenders, and bringing it to closure. Much of the early UD PIT attention has been focused heavily on reporting procedures, which is necessary to ensure the compilation of relevant baseline data that will inform other UD-related activities. As the transition to CMIS is completed and refined, other post-reporting functions will require enhanced attention because of their intrinsic importance to the UD PIT mission. For example, PIT leadership should continue to identify optimal thresholds for action, both in determining which remedial path is most appropriate and in determining a process for applying firm, fair, and reasonable sanctions for those found to have been the cause of UDs.

The Language and Guidance in Addressing UDs Are Ambiguous

The language and guidance addressing UDs are often unclear and inconsistent, which argues for the UD PIT taking steps to ensure clarity and consistency in DoD directives, manuals, and other issuances, including the UD PIT flow chart and guidance from senior officials. For example, the effort should clearly define "UD" and articulate the distinctions between truly significant UDs and those that are not. The overall UD PIT objectives would be well served by conducting a comprehensive review and revision of two DoD issuances to clarify the responsibilities of personnel regarding UDs. Each of these issuances predates the Strategic Plan:

- Enclosure 6 to DoD Manual 5200.01, Volume 3, seems widely understood as the authoritative DoD policy requirement for managing UDs, and addresses the handling of "Security Incidents Involving Classified Information."[13]
- DoD Directive (DoDD) 5210.50, "Unauthorized Disclosure of Classified Information to the Public" (July 22, 2005) is being revised with what appears to be a slightly different focus: namely,

---

[13] DoD, 2012a.

to establish a policy for the "Management of Serious Security Incidents Involving Classified Information."[14]

We believe there is long-term value in merging the policies in these two issuances to establish a "one-stop shop" for policy on handling UDs, with clear and specific guidance about the most-serious incidents. Exceptions should be clearly and unambiguously delineated, as consistent with the Strategic Plan.

For ease of use by DoD management and personnel in determining authorities and responsibilities for reporting and investigating UDs, DoDD 5210.50 should more clearly serve as the core UD policy document and should include the full range of authority at the departmental level. Consistent with standard DoD policy that gives primacy to Directives, the DoD Manual 5200.01 Enclosure 6 should derive from that Directive, rather than the other way around, as now appears to be the case in the drafting process.

The UD PIT should attempt to clarify the continuing ambiguity over reporting and investigatory obligations for cases in which there are several DoD components with an interest or equity in a particular UD (i.e., classification level and authority, mission manager, parent component of identified leaker, component where the leak occurs).

It must be made clear who in DoD has declassification authority and what declassification procedures need to be followed for authorized disclosures if classified information is considered for release to the media. Similarly, it needs to be clear how the UD PIT activities are or should be connected to the ongoing, and presumably parallel, activities of those engaged in implementing national insider threat initiatives. The similarities and differences in the obligations of current and former DoD personnel to submit materials for prepublication review also need to be spelled out.

Metrics Are Needed

While the number of UDs gets a fair amount of attention, little has been paid to those metrics that focus on results or can help with under-

---

[14] DoD, *Unauthorized Disclosure of Classified Information to the Public*, Directive 5210.50, July 22, 2005.

standing what will deter and prevent UDs. The DoD's metrics effort is still nascent. Until the UD PIT is able to deliver a richer level of detail, there will be few actionable insights that reach beyond identifying and tracking UDs. Similarly, there is a need to establish an analytic focus that addresses the causes of leaks, their consequences, and how to prevent them.

Compiling performance metrics to gauge the success of Strategic Plan implementation will rely on the reporting and tracking of cases; but metrics for the UD PIT also need to go beyond reporting and tracking to measure results that directly support detecting, deterring, and preventing UDs. Metrics will be valuable if they can help align efforts with priorities to minimize UDs.

As such, the metrics process will benefit from creating a taxonomy of UDs to facilitate the establishment of priorities, accountability, and sanctions. An effective system must identify and address the most-significant leaks to best allocate resources and establish priorities. Establishing accurate metrics is essential to determining cause and effect with regard to the effectiveness of the Strategic Plan—that is, whether the Strategic Plan is actually reducing leaks.

CI and Security Issues Are Unresolved

The UD PIT must resolve issues, ambiguities, and even resistance where CI interests arise about the obligation of all DoD elements, including CI, to formally report UDs in a timely manner to the Director of Security Policy and Oversight, OUSD(I). More-regular and improved communications between CI and security professionals—for example, through ongoing representation of each organization at the other's staff meetings—should lead to improvements in addressing these issues.

Additionally, a major security issue is the adequacy of vetting of U.S. government and contractor personnel for access to classified and sensitive information. The two recent marquee cases are former NSA contractor Edward Snowden, who defected to Russia, and Army Pfc. Bradley Manning, sentenced in court-martial proceedings to 35 years in prison for leaking. Both are responsible for significant UDs—Snowden for disclosing highly sensitive counterterrorist collection capabilities, and Manning for the disclosure of more than 700,000 classified documents to

WikiLeaks. Reportedly, both had demonstrated evidence of behavioral issues that, in retrospect, should have raised questions about their suitability for access to classified information. Any notable security "flags" should have prompted reviews of their eligibility for holding clearances and, in retrospect, probably disqualified them from access to classified information. Such a proactive security posture might have prevented the deliberate compromise of significant classified information in the headline-grabbing UDs calculated by Manning and Snowden. A successful preventive security posture will focus on insider threats of possible UDs before any act can be committed. Similarly, establishment and enforcement of such basic security measures as the two-person rule, apparently now under consideration, might also have prevented the unimpeded access that both Snowden and Manning enjoyed and the ensuing damaging disclosures.

UD Process Improvements Will Enhance Effectiveness

Organizational and management issues related to the functioning of the UD PIT require clarification and possible changes to improve direction and component responsiveness. The UD PIT leadership should assess the authority of PIT members to ensure they can obtain needed information from the components they represent to report and track UDs in the DoD-wide reporting system, as well as act on that information. This will help USD(I) facilitate the management and oversight of UD efforts, including the completion of tasks assigned in the Strategic Plan.

To ensure the timely completion of action tasks in the Strategic Plan, UD PIT leadership should assign USD(I) action officers to oversee and manage task completion by UD PIT component representatives in specific business areas (e.g., leadership, tools, training, policy). The UD PIT should also hold periodic in-person meetings to facilitate interaction and enhance oversight and accountability. Its leadership should identify which DoD security organizations and mechanisms outside the UD PIT are appropriate to ensure sufficient component insight and support for the UD PIT to implement and oversee UD matters in the longer term.

The UD PIT might enhance its reach and clout if it regularly reported to a more senior body, such as a UD forum or Steering Group that is a standing part of the DSE EXCOM. Such a senior body should meet regularly (e.g., bimonthly, quarterly) to review UD PIT actions and provide guidance and oversight. Any direct reporting connection between UD PIT members and senior Steering Group members will improve direction from above and the accountability of subordinate action officers. While the management of the UD PIT could be more assertive in assigning responsibilities to UD PIT members, we note that the management's current "light touch" approach has been adept at informing, leading by example, and perhaps at more effectively building a longer-term constituency for UD action.

The Joint Staff's ability to implement the Strategic Plan within and across the organizations under its purview seems particularly problematic. While Joint Staff UD PIT participants seem fully on board, additional drive and focus is needed, perhaps by developing additional authority relationships and the UD PIT's planned awareness briefings, to elevate the importance of the UD PIT effort and encourage greater compliance.

Because limited resources and other constraints affect UD PIT efforts, USD(I)'s Security Policy and Oversight Directorate should identify and focus UD PIT efforts on high-priority tasks, as well as more aggressively oversee and insist on membership and components being held accountable for assigned tasks.

Greater Outreach Can Leverage Gains

The UD effort has made considerable headway, and the OUSD(I) Security Policy and Oversight Directorate and, increasingly, UD PIT membership have been suitably engaged. But other major stakeholders with equities in addressing the UD problem warrant UD PIT outreach and attention. Key among these are the following:

- Other DoD organizations, such as Public Affairs, the Inspector General (IG), and Office of the General Counsel (OGC)—all of which play major UD roles but are effectively outside the span of USD(I) control

- ODNI, where all DoD intelligence components have overlapping authorities as members of the IC
- The White House and NSC staff, where government-wide UD issues and correctives overlap with those of DoD
- Congress, where both the intelligence and armed services committees are also wrestling with how to improve the U.S. government's performance in stemming UDs, including through draft legislation
- External organizations such as the Information Security Oversight Office (ISOO), where classification and declassification issues highlight perennial problems associated with secrecy and transparency.

CHAPTER THREE

Recommendations

The recommendations offered in this report are keyed on sustaining the successes that the UD PIT has already achieved. They also seek to enhance and focus UD PIT efforts to address any uncompleted actions, shortfalls, and other areas of the DoD UD Strategic Plan that warrant priority attention. They are designed to present a holistic approach to consolidating the task-oriented focus and implementation of the Strategic Plan. Where appropriate, we selectively incorporate some of the observations from Chapter Two into the relevant recommendations for clarity and coherence. Here, we present 22 recommendations, spread across the categories of UD PIT management, culture and accountability, policy and new initiatives, and studies and outreach.

UD PIT Management

1. **Hold your ground.** *Revalidate the Strategic Plan and the importance of the UD PIT, and maintain and consolidate the gains already established by the UD PIT in implementing the Strategic Plan.* The key here is to not lose momentum or give observers or possible detractors any basis to suspect that the UD effort may coast, lose importance, or face a decline in OSD priorities. For example, a third USD(I) memo in the UD series should direct the reporting transition from SIR to CMIS. This would allow an opportunity to provide a more expansive validation by the USD(I) and the new Secretary of Defense. It is also important to inventory the gains and work to ensure their sustainability,

especially the longer-term sustainability of the UD infrastructure and its members.

2. **Expand your ground.** *Grow the UD initiative through a recalibrated and even more ambitious agenda, and through greater DoD-wide senior-level oversight and direction.* It is important to understand the initial gains of the UD PIT as being preliminary, getting a foothold on slippery terrain. Having established the beachhead, momentum counts: Now is the time to gain new ground, not just hold initial gains. This should involve taking inventory of unfinished business and prioritizing the effort to ensure visible accomplishments.

3. **Sustain the top-down approach.** *With the transition in Defense Secretaries, ensure that the top-level priority and support assigned to the UD initiative by the previous Secretary is reinforced and sustained by the new Secretary and his leadership team.* For example, any statement of new Secretary of Defense priorities should ideally include UD prevention and deterrence, accountability for personnel and management, and the need to change the leaks-tolerant culture. The USD(I) should periodically reiterate this message.

4. **Enhance UD PIT authority.** *Empower UD PIT members within their components and establish a SES-level UD steering group— possibly as an arm or subgroup of the DSE EXCOM—to which the UD PIT should regularly report.* The PIT will experience greater success if it is given enhanced clout and oversight. This can be achieved by assigning visible and meaningful authorities and accountability for UD PIT members within their own components, as well as through other UD process improvements described in Chapter Two. Establishing a standing SES-level UD steering group could also support this enhancement: The group could lend additional authority to the working-level UD process in disparate DoD elements because of its greater seniority and separate reporting chains to its senior members. Particular emphasis and support needs to be given to the Joint Staff in bringing the combatant commands fully aboard the DoD's UD prevention efforts. Additional actions that will enhance UD

PIT authority include the continued successful implementation of the UD Strategic Plan and the implementation of the recommendations in this report, especially Recommendation 3—reinforcing the top-down approach and seeking the full authority of the new Secretary of Defense.

5.   **Focus on the significant UDs.** *With prioritization guidance worked out by the Program Management Office (PMO), direct the UD PIT's focus to the most serious disclosures of leaks to the media.* Not all UDs are equally important. Some are only infractions or minor violations, while others are extremely serious. In addition to implementing the Strategic Plan's priority tasks, assign priority energy and resources to seeing significant leak events through the complete accountability process, leaving the less important UDs for more routine security attention.

6.   **Establish metrics to track results.** *After reporting numbers of UDs, a more granular system of categorizing UDs and tracking end-to-end results is needed to better evaluate the performance of the UD PIT and PMO in accomplishing their missions.* Close tracking of case ownership, leaker identification and accountability, and the application of sanctions will present a fuller picture that allows better evaluation of DoD's achievements, undone work, and shortcomings in addressing UDs.

Culture and Accountability

7.   **Connect culture change with UD results.** *Establish full UD accountability by identifying leakers and applying sanctions.* This is necessary to help change the mindset that leaking classified information to the media is permissible conduct for which one will not be caught or held accountable. This culture of permissibility will not change until the disincentives to leaking outweigh the incentives of doing so. Moreover, stopping, reporting, and investigating leaks must be seen as part of the mission rather than as a distraction to the mission.

8. **Ensure end-to-end accountability for results.** *The UD PIT should ensure that full ownership of every serious UD is assumed or assigned, that accountability is established as offenders are identified and adjudicated, and that appropriate sanctions are implemented before any serious case is brought to closure.* This means moving the effort from identifying and reporting UDs to the next phases of the end-to-end process: taking ownership, establishing accountability, and applying sanctions.

9. **Energize the three-track system.** *Ensure that accountability is established by clarifying policies, directives, and guidance to help managers understand their authorities and responsibilities.* Once identified, UD offenders must face consequences for violations. All should be channeled, in a timely fashion, to one or more levels of sanctions, beginning with administrative measures, ascending to civil penalties where appropriate, and to criminal prosecution in the most serious cases. The UD policies and processes must be clear in how this channeling happens and how to optimize its results.[1]

10. **Facilitate compliance through a reasonable approach.** *To be effective, the system must facilitate, not inhibit, compliance. Therefore, the consequences of UD violations must be visible, meaningful, and fair.* This means that publication review must be timely; requirements to protect information must be seen as reasonable and not unduly burdensome; and accountability measures must be fair and applied consistently. To be effective, departmental and component awareness and education efforts must communicate the intent, rationale, and results of these efforts. This approach will require distinct but related communications and awareness training plans (Recommendation 11). If the workforce gains confidence in the new rules and is assured that the rules will be enforced evenly and fairly, the chances for favorable culture change will improve appreciably.

11. **Prioritize and deliver quality UD training and education.** *Enhanced training and awareness are necessary to change the*

---

[1]   See Appendix A for a discussion of thresholds for taking legal action against leakers.

culture and inculcate responsibilities in support of the goals of the Strategic Plan. A workforce that is more knowledgeable and alert to UDs will improve compliance and support culture change. Such a workforce will be more fully aware of the rules and rationale for acceptable conduct, of what is permissible and what is not, and of what the penalties are for UD offenses. Effective UD training should include a specific DoD-wide communications plan that will reach the many thousands of department employees who might never receive formal UD awareness training. Both communications and training initiatives should elevate department-wide situational awareness and better compliance with laws and regulations governing the protection and disclosure of classified information.

More in-depth training should cover the following:

- requirements and authorities for classification and declassification, including the negative consequences of inconsistent and over-classification
- the restrictions governing and the harm caused by "authorized leaks" that undermine accountability and the integrity of the system
- the damage that leaks do to military operations and plans, defense preparedness, and intelligence sources and methods
- how these losses impair national and DoD decision advantage and degrade mission effectiveness in both policy and warfighter support.

Meaningful training for all SES-level and working-level personnel and contractors should be the goal, and this training should use technologies that support online training and testing capabilities, with certification of completion mandatory. Such training could be included in a broader security training and awareness effort, with a clearly delineated segment addressing UDs. Greater emphasis should also be placed on ensuring compliance by DoD components in the ODNI's Sensitive Compartmented Information (SCI)-level training.

Policy and New Initiatives

12. **Align UD language with PIT goals.** *Ensure language clarity and consistency in all relevant DoD documents, directives, manuals and official issuances, and the full range of departmental authorities.* UD efforts must be supported by directives and guidance that are easy to locate and understand, are not unduly cumbersome or burdensome, and facilitate compliance. Ambiguities are especially apparent about UD definitions, declassification authorities, pre- and postpublication review, requirements for approval of official and nonofficial publication, distinctions in the obligations of current and former employees, and authorities and limitations regarding interactions with the media. In addition, the timing of and details about UD reporting, including reporting on sensitive matters, is ambiguous or difficult to discern.

    These policies and directives should be revised for clarity, especially DoD Directive 5210.50 (as the policy document governing disclosures to the public), and DoD Manual 5200.01-V3, Enclosure 6. Particular emphasis should be put on requirements pertaining to serious security incidents, but the Directive would be even more useful if it were a "one-stop shop" for all DoD policy on UDs, with disclosures to the media and other serious disclosures duly covered as a subset. The Manual's obligations with respect to UDs should more explicitly derive from the Directive, and the current, ongoing review and update process should capture relevant memos and statements issued by the Secretary and on his behalf by the USD(I) and the Director of Public Affairs, to ensure the mandates from such items survive.

13. **Resolve classification and sensitivity barriers.** *Ensure that, regardless of sensitivity, UDs involving issues with CI, IG, law enforcement, SCI, Special Access Program (SAP), and Alternative Compensatory Control Measures (ACCM) are reported in a timely manner to the Security Policy and Oversight Directorate.* There is a need to ensure appropriate, secure transparency about UD events and more effective mitigation of potential damage.

Appropriate transparency is needed to affirm the integrity of UD reporting statistics. Timely reporting also helps ensure that UD events are addressed not only from an investigatory and component perspective but also from a DoD-wide security and UD perspective, thus mitigating damage that could result if the UD is not promptly communicated to security. Further integration of security and CI personnel will improve collaboration and reporting. Consider creating a rotational placement for a security officer in CI and a CI officer in security to enhance collaboration and two-way transparency. At a minimum, officers from CI and security components should regularly attend each other's staff meetings.

14. **Review security vetting for classified access.** *The UD PIT should elevate the importance of such security measures in its Strategic Plan that will help it lead an effort to review and reform the DoD personnel security vetting procedures to help prevent the clearing of potential future leakers such as Snowden and Manning for classified access, or suspend their clearances if questionable conduct warrants it.* U.S. government and contractor personnel should not be cleared for access to classified and sensitive information without undergoing a thorough vetting process that includes a reliable and predictive evaluation of security trustworthiness. Predictive models for precisely who will breach security rules, break laws, and compromise significant classified information can never be perfect. But background investigations and security adjudications that do not reveal or act on information that should be a disqualifier for privileged access, or that fail to act on new information that bears on trustworthiness, represent serious flaws in the gateway to sensitive information, which requires better protection than it is currently afforded.

15. **Leverage technology.** *Review available technologies and develop or adapt new technologies to enhance the implementation of the Strategic Plan and other UD initiatives for training, analytic, and investigatory purposes, as well as for protecting information and systems.* The UD PIT, in collaboration with the Chief Information Officer and others, should explore effective uses of technol-

ogy to help prevent leaks and identify leakers. This will be particularly important as the development of the Joint Information Environment proceeds and increasing demands for mobility, interoperability, and cloud computing demand increased identities management and approaches that manage risk rather than avoid it. It will be wise to incorporate technology use at the development stage, not just after deployment.

16. **Lay the foundation for the enactment of comprehensive leaks legislation.** *Identify promising attributes of more effective laws addressing UDs, brief the Armed Services and Intelligence Committees on the Strategic Plan and its implementation, and gauge and build support from those committees, the White House, and others for submitting draft leaks legislation for consideration.* While the political climate for some kind of leaks law reform is more favorable now than it has been in recent years, such a climate by no means ensures success in enacting legislative relief, and the prospect of investigations of the press have led to calls for shield laws. Still, both intelligence committees, the House Permanent Select Committee on Intelligence (HPSCI) and the Senate Select Committee on Intelligence (SSCI), have recently been receptive to constructive suggestions on how to improve the laws addressing leaks of classified information.

Legislative measures that could be considered include new provisions distinct from the espionage laws for those who violated their secrecy obligations, as well as provisions carefully tailored to apply to others who may not have the same obligations but who also disclose classified information. For example, in much the same way that acting with a reckless disregard for what is true or false can give rise to a defamation action without harm to First Amendment rights, there is merit in enabling civil sanctions (as opposed to criminal ones) against someone who publishes classified information with gross negligence or a reckless disregard for the damage such disclosures can cause to national security.

Implementing the Strategic Plan will be essential to persuading Congress that DoD has done all it can do without congressional assistance. Showing that DoD took concerted steps to "clean its own house first" will likely increase support for better leaks laws that more clearly explicate illegal conduct and strengthen the enforceability of sanctions for leaks.

Studies and Outreach

17. **Conduct a comprehensive study of UDs.** *A comprehensive study should assess the causes, consequences, and correctives that will help in understanding UDs, prioritizing efforts, and sustaining the effectiveness of the UD program over the long haul.* The current approach is based more on an intuitive or anecdotal understanding of UDs than an empirical one. While appropriate for getting the effort started, such an approach is insufficient to produce durable results. Sustaining effectiveness over the longer haul, particularly in light of dwindling resources and the need to prioritize, requires a more solid understanding of the UD causes, consequences, and correctives.

    A comprehensive study should build a database and develop a taxonomy of UDs that: identifies criteria for the most important categories; focuses on the motivations of leakers (i.e., who leaks and why); identifies which kinds of sensitive sources, methods, and operations are most fragile and perishable if exposed; develops metrics to assess the damage caused by UDs; establishes causal connections between press leaks and harm to intelligence and military capabilities, including leaks' audit-trail case studies; explores the implications of technology in light of WikiLeaks and cyber capabilities; and assesses the relative effectiveness or ineffectiveness of the extant penalties regime.

18. **Study ways to improve the identification of leakers (Step 3 of the end-to-end accountability process).** *Review available analytic, technological, collaborative, and investigatory tools and authorities and develop new tools to identify leakers, including when investigative elements decline to pursue an investigation.* Appreciably reducing leaks will require better success in iden-

tifying leakers. UD investigations conducted by security, CI, IG, and law enforcement elements require substantial improvements in identifying offenders who escape detection because of constraints inherent in the DoJ's Eleven Questions process, journalists' ability to shield anonymous government sources, and Attorney General guidelines inhibiting investigations that target journalists. Leakers cannot be held accountable if they cannot be identified. For those cases in which the Federal Bureau of Investigation (FBI) or DoJ decline investigation or prosecution, the USD(I) should determine if further effort is warranted to attempt to identify the leaker or, if the leaker has been identified, to ensure that appropriate administrative steps are taken (see Step 4).

19. **Study ways to improve the ability to implement sanctions when leakers are identified (Step 4 of the end-to-end accountability process).** *The three-track sanction options— administrative, civil, and criminal—should be closely reviewed for application and effectiveness.* Barriers to applying sanctions should be identified and removed or mitigated, and areas for improvement should be highlighted and prioritized for action. The review should include an examination of the DoD decisionmaking process on whether to pursue legal action against identified leakers, and should formulate recommendations for personnel evaluation mechanisms to link human resources (HR) personnel to the sanctions process. Greater HR engagement should help establish clear responsibilities for administering sanctions and ensuring consistency in their application to inspire confidence that the system is rational and fair.

20. **Expand outreach.** *The UD PIT should take advantage of the expertise and lessons learned from the numerous organizations outside USD(I) that have interests and equities in supporting or impeding the UD PIT goals.* The PMO and PIT leadership and staff should reach out more concertedly to:
    ◦ ODNI, IC agencies, and CI elements, where UDs are a major concern but authorities overlap

- the White House and NSC staff, where broad oversight of UD issues may support improved interagency cooperation in a U.S. government-wide effort
- Congress, where both intelligence and armed services committees are seeking improvements in U.S. government performance in stemming UDs and better laws to control leaks
- other DoD organizations with UD engagement, such as Public Affairs, the IG, and the OGC
- such external organizations as the ISOO, where classification issues highlight perennial problems associated with secrecy, disclosures, and transparency.

Additionally, outreach should include consultations with ISOO and others to address authorities and practices about authorized DoD disclosures of national intelligence and other disclosures to the media and to the public that could be perceived as "authorized leaks." Specific outreach to public affairs offices is essential, given their direct media contacts that require decisions on whether to support or prevent the publication of classified information by "confirming" leaked information held by journalists and others who may not have the necessary security clearances to access that leaked information. Specific policy changes addressing both information security and public affairs should seek improvements and consistency in this complex and risky process.

In due course, the UD PIT should also spearhead an outreach effort to raise awareness and educate policy officials in other (non-DoD) agencies about their obligations to protect classified DoD information and the damage that can result if those obligations are ignored. A robust outreach program should eventually engage civil libertarians (e.g., the American Civil Liberties Union), constitutional lawyers, academics, and the journalist-media community. Such outreach could generate better mutual understanding and help identify areas where overlapping equities may foster greater agreement on mitigating the harm that UDs cause to U.S. security, as well as better ways—including perhaps better laws—to protect sensitive information from public disclosure.

21. **Seek closer alignment with the ODNI and other IC approaches to UDs.** *As a matter of good organizational alignment, ensure that separate IC and DoD action tracks are appropriately synchronized with each other.* Doing so will help ensure that no UD can fall through the IC/DoD cracks. Also, review whether DoD should adopt some of the IC's best practices about UD processes and procedures. Since all DoD intelligence elements are simultaneously members of the IC, many of them, including the national agencies—National Security Agency (NSA), National Geospatial-Intelligence Agency (NGA), Defense Intelligence Agency (DIA), and National Reconnaissance Office (NRO)—may identify their UD responsibilities and processes more closely with the IC than with DoD. Improved IC synchronization will require closer bilateral relationships with individual intelligence agencies—including the CIA—on UD processes and specific serious cases, as well as working more closely with the ODNI.

22. **Engage the Inspectors General.** *The role of the IG in supporting the top-down initiative should be better defined, with particular emphasis on identifying systemic problems in the implementation of the Strategic Plan and other UD-related mechanisms, practices, and shortcomings, as well as emphasizing investigations in which IG authorities may be valuable in crossing organizational lines.* The role of the IG should not be limited to participating in investigations to identify leakers. IG offices can play a significant role in identifying systemic problems in implementing the Strategic Plan, identifying leakers in situations for which IG authorities may be needed to cross organizational lines, assessing systems for imposing sanctions, and identifying security deficiencies and lessons learned during routine and other component inspections that can help other components and DoD-wide UD efforts.

Thresholds for Taking Legal Action Against Leakers

This appendix briefly summarizes discussions with UD PIT leadership about determining thresholds for taking legal actions against a leaker of classified information. The basic issue is how to determine when to prosecute for UDs as opposed to taking other actions or no action at all. In brief, determining sanctions for UDs has to be addressed on a case-by-case basis, while bearing the following considerations in mind:

1. **What is the damage to U.S. national security?** The answer to this question will require input from analysts and operational and security experts and is an early and key factor in considering a course of action. Intelligence cases would require a good demonstration of irreparable, costly, or difficult-to-recover damage to sources and methods or to operations. The metrics for assessing this damage are problematic, typically classified, and thus tricky to use in court. This issue emphasizes developing systematic criteria for assigning importance to particular cases.[1]

2. **What was the person's intent?** Certainly, when considering court action, intent is important to meet the statutory criteria to determine if a law has been violated.[2] Without establishing intent, a prosecution will not likely succeed.

---

[1] Of particular note for DoD information, prosecutions can be complicated further because of distinctions between *defense information*, the term used in the espionage laws dating to 1917, and *national security information*, the more recent descriptor for classified information.

[2] See, generally, Title 18 of the U.S. Code including sections 793 and 794, commonly referred to as the "espionage laws." For example, the prosecution was not able to establish intent in the Manning case regarding the charge of aiding the enemy, although even the

3. **What options are available?** There are essentially three levels of sanctions, each with their own pros and cons. We present these levels in ascending order of how severe they are and how difficult they are to apply:

- **administrative sanctions**; e.g., reprimand, loss of pay, suspension of security clearances; reassignment, demotion, or termination of employment.
- **civil litigation**, such as the *Marchetti* and *Snepp* cases, brought for violations of secrecy agreements and efforts to seek book royalties—a similar, more recent case involving a CIA officer using the pseudonym Ishmael Jones was a big win for the government that reaffirmed *Snepp* (like Snepp, Jones had not properly gone through CIA's pre-publication review process).[3]
- **criminal prosecution**, such as the *Morison* case in 1985 (prosecution for disclosing imagery to a foreign trade journal) and the more recent *Kiriakou* case (prosecution for disclosing the identities of covert CIA employees).[4]

Notably, an obligation to protect national security information exists regardless of the existence of a nondisclosure agreement because the obligation is a matter of trust and may be implicit as well explicit.[5] Establishing a historical database of past actions would provide a useful guide for determining the options avail-

---

defense agreed that the evidence submitted by the prosecution showing Al Qaeda exploitation of WikiLeaks materials was factual. See David Dishneau and Pauline Jelinek, "Al-Qaeda Sought to Benefit from WikiLeaks Documents, Prosecutors Say," *Washington Post*, July 1, 2013, p. 1.

[3] *United States v. Marchetti*, 466 F. 2d 1309, 4th Circuit, 1972, cert. denied, 409 U.S. 1063, 1972; *Snepp v. United States*, 1980; *United States v. Ishmael Jones*, 2012. *Snepp* and *Jones* support the proposition that the government could obtain the proceeds from sales of a book that the author failed to submit for prepublication review.

[4] *United States v. Morison*, 1988; *United States v. John C. Kiriakou*, 2013.

[5] See *United States v. Marchetti*, 1972. The decision upheld a CIA secrecy agreement. The court stated that an obligation "probably" would be implied even in the absence of an agreement.

able for future actions, because such a database would help counter arguments of inconsistency and unfair treatment.

Of course, recommending a prosecution does not necessarily mean that DoJ will agree to bring a case, and there are many reasons why it might object. An important reason is first-time disclosure: If there are prior disclosures about the sources and methods of interest, for example, the burden of proof that there has been additional damage caused by the leaker may be difficult to demonstrate, and DoJ will not want to bring a case it may lose.

- In criminal cases, a leaker might not be seen as an appropriate target in the eyes of the press or jurors, who may determine, depending on the circumstances, that prosecution under the espionage laws seems overly harsh. Because the United States has no comprehensive leaks statute, prosecutions tend to be under the more difficult—and eyebrow-raising—espionage laws or as theft of government property or more narrowly focused law, because leaks to the media are understandably not seen as espionage.[6]
- In civil cases, less serious civil actions for violating an agreement or other trust do not trigger the same level of concern but would still raise interest from the press. Again, each case will be different.

4. **What are the implications of prosecuting?** There are implications if the government seeks to prosecute, as well as if it does nothing.
   - Prosecutions can risk public disclosure of sensitive or classified information during the courts process, which could cause even more damage than the initial UD, depend-

---

[6] In addition, specific and narrowly drawn laws criminalize the disclosure of the identities of covert CIA employees and agents (U.S. Code, Title 50, section 421 et. seq. "Protection of Identities of Certain United States Undercover Intelligence Officers, Agents, Informants, and Sources") and the disclosure of classified information about cryptologic systems and communications intelligence activities (U.S. Code, Title 18, section 798, "Disclosure of Classified Information").

ing on the circumstances. The Classified Information Procedures Act (CIPA) can mitigate some, but not all, of the damage that could result from proceeding, and the government must determine if proceeding is worth the anticipated costs. However, if successful, both criminal and civil cases almost certainly advance the cause of stemming leaks much more effectively than do lesser sanctions.

- ○ Losing the case is also a risk because it could set back efforts and momentum to get a better legal grip on this problem.
- ○ Doing nothing may send a troubling signal that the government is powerless to hold leakers accountable, thus encouraging further violations. The early angst over the *No Easy Day* controversy illustrates this dilemma.

Thus, each possible action has its own pros and cons depending on the situation, and these must be assessed carefully at the outset as policymakers decide which action to take, with input from managers, analysts, operations and security personnel, legal counsel, press officers, and others.

Leaks Questions and Responses

This appendix provides responses to four specific questions posed by OUSD(I) Security during the project about leaking by senior officials, overclassification and proving damage, freedom-of-press issues, and intrusive measures to monitor employee conduct.

1. **Some feel that our precedent in allowing senior officials/ officers to break the rules without negative action inhibits the department from taking action against more junior/ midcareer personnel.**

    This need not logically follow, but public perceptions when dealing with enforcement issues can be a practical inhibitor. Regardless of whether this has been true in the past, taking appropriate action against senior-level officers can break such a pattern and mindset. The consistent enforcement of punishment for rule violations will support the goals of the Strategic Plan.

    Personnel generally will understand actions that appear fair and reasonable (i.e., the punishment fits the crime), so processes designed to avoid arbitrary or inconsistent sanctions are important. For example, intentional acts (e.g., deliberate disclosures) should be treated more severely than unintentional acts (e.g., a lack of discipline or care), and a range of penalties (oral warnings, written reprimands, suspension, dismissal, etc.) is preferable to a one-size-fits-all approach. Personnel security, or other bodies that oversee or serve as a resource for determining penalties, can help ensure greater consistency in this regard and provide guidance while also recognizing any mitigating circumstances that may justify what could be perceived as inconsistent treatment (e.g., lack of training or supervision, repeated carelessness).

One important factor in sending the right message will be how DoD publicizes sanctions, and legal offices will have to be engaged to ensure compliance with privacy requirements. For example, a written announcement that identifies the violations, grade levels of the personnel involved, and sanctions without identifying the actors specifically may be appropriate in most cases. As an illustration, the FBI's Office of Professional Responsibility (OPR) sends quarterly memos to the entire workforce summarizing violations of laws and rules by its employees and indicating the sanctions applied, along with mitigating and aggravating factors. The names of offenders are not publicized, but the message is clear: If caught, you will be held accountable.

2. **Another argument is that the information shouldn't be classified to begin with or is already the worst-kept secret in government. We know what the policy says, but the practical reality is that leaders shy away from taking action because of concern that "damage" might be hard to prove.**

Training and education on proper classification and handling are important and may help reduce overclassification. It should also sensitize personnel to the need to avoid discussing information that appears publicly and without authority because of unauthorized disclosures. A key action item in the Strategic Plan addresses classification management, and improvement in classification decisions is an important vehicle for addressing this concern. Still, regardless of the details, the issue involves discipline and breach of trust, and violations of the rules must continue to be addressed administratively as such; there is no need to show damage, except to determine the severity of the sanction.

However, the concern over having to show damage is an important factor when attempting to prepare a case for criminal prosecution, and the availability of the information in the public domain can make it more difficult to prove the case as a practical if not legal matter. This is often compounded if proving the damage results in publication of even more revealing information than was initially involved. Assuming the culprit is known and the damage is real, there are ways to mitigate the damage concerns.

First, DoD could take administrative steps against even former employees, including, for example, the denial of contracts or security clearances. Actions taken for violations of DoD requirements need not show damage; they can be justified by a lack of trustworthiness and suitability for employment/clearance. Second, DoD could pursue civil action for the violation of nondisclosure agreements. These actions require showing merely a failure to submit the information for review and do not require that damage be shown. There is ample case law to support such actions. Third, criminal prosecution is an appropriate route that does not always require showing damaging disclosures to a foreign enemy, depending on the nature of the offense. But attempting to proceed against someone suspected of leaking to the public without the ability to show harm to national defense, as provided in the espionage laws, can present a psychological barrier (at least to those who argue that leakers are not spies) and thus a practical obstacle to a successful case.

For this reason, a comprehensive approach to dealing with unauthorized disclosures should include not only aggressive internal DoD measures but also steps to build a consensus in the public sector (executive and legislative branches) and private sector (defense industry, academia, media) for appropriate but comprehensive legislation to control UDs—an approach that is based on the premise that leaks are violations of law, the public trust, and other specific regulations, but are not espionage.

Such efforts would have to show that even effective DoD programs have their limitations and that leaks legislation—with both civil and criminal remedies—is narrowly shaped to cover those who intentionally violate their obligations not to reveal classified information.

3. **A most frustrating type of UD is media leaks. As you are very much aware, anyone with an axe to grind might determine that it is his/her responsibility to divulge classified information to the public. I put "political leakers" into the same category. Our ability to tackle the "press" side of the leak is justifiably constrained by the Bill of Rights. Under what circumstances are these constraints lifted or otherwise mitigated by other law?**

Addressing the challenges of dealing with the press involves substantial legal review, as well as analysis of policy and practical considerations. Attorney General guidelines establish specific restrictions on law enforcement actions against journalists and the press. Comprehensive leaks legislation could further clarify freedom-of-press boundaries about publishing classified information, and it is noteworthy that even some press representatives may be receptive to the notion of more narrowly crafted laws to deal with the need to protect national security. For example, the media's support for enacting legislation that criminalized the disclosure of covert identities of undercover personnel resulted from the statute's limitation on actions against the press. The key exception to this was a provision aimed at those engaged in a "pattern or practice" of revealing covert identities, such as the UK-based Covert Action Bulletin (later learned to be KGB-funded), whose main purpose was specifically to compromise CIA operations and officers under cover. A more comprehensive leaks law that takes a similarly nuanced approach or perhaps a civil action based on showing gross negligence or a reckless disregard of any damaging consequences caused by publication might provide a workable framework, particularly when dealing with WikiLeaks-type disclosures and other disclosures that are not seen as traditional espionage.

Dealing with the so-called legitimate press is more challenging but is not an insurmountable problem. First, taking steps to identify a leaker by obtaining information from the press requires a combination of political will and a thorough exhaustion of available steps within government. Of course, this assumes the information at issue is truly damaging, because a court is less likely to support intrusion on press rights without the demonstration of such harm. The use of search warrants and subpoenas can be an effective legal tool in the right cases, because the press is not automatically immune.

Steps can also be taken against the press for violation of the law under the right circumstances, as we noted about the Identities Act, and there is already precedent for action against those who release to the press classified information that was stolen from government (e.g., the Morison case).

However, no measures against the press will succeed unless DoD can show that it has taken all appropriate steps internally to stop leaks, protect its information, and address overclassification, and that it has reached the limits of its investigatory powers so that actions involving the press can be viewed as the only remaining recourse. An effort to engage the press on this point will be important, as will the preparation of legislation that does not attempt to overreach.

In addition, steps to deal with media leaks will generate public support if they are seen as reasonably tailored to information that is actually damaging when leaked and not designed to impede free speech on legitimate issues of public concern.

Finally, an effective mechanism for addressing and publicizing whistleblower concerns would help eliminate the belief that leakers have no other recourse.

4. **In the same vein, how intrusive might we be in observing the behaviors of employees on and off the job to determine risk and establish guilt, etc.? How do we create a better legal environment for monitoring these behaviors appropriately? (I'm thinking primarily of behaviors online.)**

This is a risk management issue. It is unrealistic to think that all leaks can be stopped or identified, and there are resource issues involved in trying. Establishing an aggressive identities management program is one way to monitor online behavior involving the use of DoD systems so that, for example, unusual patterns could be identified. Steps to preclude the downloading of data, prohibit the use of thumb drives, and limit and monitor data transfers can all reduce the risk of unauthorized disclosures. Some agencies have a "dirty word" search program they use to identify classified leaks. Collaboration between security, IT, CI, human resources, public affairs, and legal officers is essential to arrive at solutions. It is important that the steps taken are part of a comprehensive program that is understood and seen as reasonable.

Observation of personnel in the workplace is governed by a variety of legal requirements, and what DoD can do depends on the purpose of the activity; for example, whether a criminal investigation is involved will determine if a warrant for surveillance is required. Taking steps to identify specific leakers (e.g., through document identification and control measures) may also be warranted, depending on the circumstances. Adequate notice to personnel that their on-site/online behavior is being monitored can satisfy many of the legal requirements. Rewarding those who report improper activity can also help identify leakers, but care must be taken to avoid creating a backlash to what might be seen as overly intrusive government conduct to encourage "snitching," because this could undermine more accepted security practices.

As previously noted, a fair and reasonable disciplinary program can be an effective tool that encourages compliance, and the identification and sanction of senior culprits can provide a degree of *in terrorem* benefit (i.e., enhanced deterrence)—a specific goal of the UD Strategic Plan.

Bibliography

Literature and Commentary

Abel, Elie, *Leaking: Who Does It? Who Benefits at What Cost?* New York: Priority Press Publications, 1987.

Ballou, Eric E., and Kyle E. McSlarrow, "Plugging the Leak: A Case for Legislative Resolution of the Conflict Between Demands of Secrecy and the Need for an Open Government," *Virginia Law Review*, June 1985, pp. 801–868.

Bruce, James B., "Laws and Leaks of Classified Intelligence: The Consequences of Permissive Neglect," *Studies in Intelligence*, Vol. 47, No. 1, March 2003, pp. 39–49.

———, "How Leaks of Classified Intelligence Help U.S. Adversaries: Implications for Laws and Secrecy," in Roger Z. George and Roger D. Kline, eds., *Intelligence and the National Security Strategist: Enduring Issues and Challenges*, Washington, D.C.: National Defense University Press, 2004, pp. 399–414.

———, "The Impact on Foreign Denial and Deception of Increased Availability of Public Information about U.S. Intelligence," in Roy Godson and James J. Wirtz (eds.), *Strategic Denial and Deception: The Twenty-First Century Challenge,* New Brunswick, N.J.: Transaction Pub. Co., 2001, pp. 229–240.

Dishneau, David, and Pauline Jelinek, "Al-Qaeda Sought to Benefit from WikiLeaks Documents, Prosecutors Say," *Washington Post*, July 1, 2013.

Edgar, Harold, and Benno C. Schmidt, "The Espionage Statues and the Publication of Defense Information," *Columbia Law Review,* Vol. 73, No. 5, May 1973, pp. 929–1087.

Gerstein, Josh, "Feds: Leaking Is Worse than Spying," *Politico*, January 17, 2011. As of February 15, 2013:
http://www.politico.com/blogs/joshgerstein/0111/Feds_leaking_is_worse_than_spying.html

Ignatius, David, "When Does Blowing Secrets Cross the Line?" *Washington Post*, July 2, 2000, p. B7.

Jameson, W. George, "Safeguarding National Security Information: Dealing with Unauthorized Disclosures of Classified Information," *Conference Reports: "National Security, Law in a Changed World: The Twelfth Annual Review of the Field,"* American Bar Association, *National Security Law Report*, Vol. 25, No. 1, May 2003.

Keller, Bill, "The Boy Who Kicked the Hornet's Nest," *The New York Times Magazine*, January 30, 2011, p. 32ff.

Kirchick, James, "Wikileaks' Collateral Damage," *The Wall Street Journal*, December 31, 2010, p. A11.

Kube, Courtney, Matthew DeLuca, and Erin McClam, "'I'm Sorry That I Hurt the United States': Bradley Manning Apologizes in Court," NBCNews.com, August 14, 2013. As of August 16, 2013:
http://usnews.nbcnews.com/_news/2013/08/14/20020933-im-sorry-that-i-hurt-the-united-states-bradley-manning-apologizes-in-court

Mitchell, Greg, "Why WikiLeaks Matters," *The Nation*, January 13, 2011. As of February 15, 2013:
http://www.thenation.com/article/157729/why-wikileaks-matters#

Ross, Gary, *Who Watches the Watchmen: The Conflict Between National Security and Freedom of the Press*, Washington, D.C.: National Intelligence Press, 2011.

Schoenfeld, Gabriel, "Has the *New York Times* Violated the Espionage Act?" *Commentary*, March 2006, pp. 22–31.

———, *Necessary Secrets: National Security, the Media, and the Rule of Law*, New York: W.W. Norton, 2010.

Waters, Clay, "Public Editor Recants: *Times* Was Wrong to Expose Terrorist Surveillance Program," *TimesWatch, Media Research Center*, October 23, 2006. As of February 15, 2013:
http://www.mrc.org/articles/
public-editor-recants-times-was-wrong-expose-terrorist-surveillance-program

Washington Post Editorial Board, "Not Every Leak Is Tantamount to Treason," *Washington Post*, August 1, 2013.

U.S. Government Documents

Ashcroft, John, "Report to the Speaker of the House of Representatives in Compliance with Section 310 of the Intelligence Authorization Act for Fiscal Year 2002" [Ashcroft Report on Leaks], October 15, 2002.

Commission on the Intelligence Capabilities of the United States Regarding Weapons of Mass Destruction, *Report to the President of the United States* [Silberman-Robb WMD Commission Report], Washington, D.C.: U.S. Government Printing Office, 2005.

Commission on Protecting and Reducing Government Secrecy, *Report of the Commission on Protecting and Reducing Government Secrecy* [Moynihan Report], S. Report 105-2, Washington, D.C.: U.S. Government Printing Office, March 3, 1997.

National Counterintelligence Policy Board, *Report to the NSC on Unauthorized Media Leak Disclosures*, March 1996.

Report of the Interdepartmental Group on Unauthorized Disclosures of Classified Information [Willard Report], March 31, 1982.

U.S. House of Representatives, *Espionage Laws and Leaks Hearing Before the Subcommittee on Legislation of the House Permanent Select Committee on Intelligence*, 96th Congress 1st Session 22, 1979.

Court Cases

Central Intelligence Agency v. Sims, 471 U.S. 159, 1985.

Snepp v. United States, U.S. Supreme Court, 444 U.S. 507, February 19, 1980.

United States v. Ishmael Jones, U.S. District Court for the Eastern District of Virginia, Alexandria Division, Case 1:10-cv-00765-GBL-TRJ, 2012.

United States v. John C. Kiriakou, U.S. District Court for the Eastern District of Virginia, Alexandria Division, Case 1:12-cr-00127-001, January 23, 2013.

United States v. Marchetti, 466 F. 2d 1309, 4th Circuit, 1972, cert. denied, 409 U.S. 1063, 1972.

United States v. Morison, United States Court of Appeals for the 4th Circuit, 844 F.2d 1057, April 1, 1988.

Selected Laws, Policies, and Directives

Bush, George W., "Memorandum for the Heads of Executive Departments and Agencies, Designation and Sharing of Controlled Unclassified Information (CUI)," 2008.

Director of National Intelligence, *Security Policy Directive for Unauthorized Disclosure of Classified Information*, Intelligence Community Directive 701, March 14, 2007.

————, *Discovery and Dissemination or Retrieval of Information within the Intelligence Community*, Intelligence Community Directive 501, January 21, 2009.

————, "Intelligence Community Reporting and Investigation of Unauthorized Disclosures of Classified Information," memorandum, May 7, 2011.

————, *Protection of National Intelligence*, Intelligence Community Directive 700, June 7, 2012.

DoD—*See* U.S. Departmnt of Defense.

Federal Register, *ISOO Directive No. 1*, Vol. 60, No. 198, October 13, 1995.

Public Law 112-277, Intelligence Authorization Act for Fiscal Year 2013, Section 504, January 14, 2013.

Under Secretary of Defense for Intelligence, "Clarification of Policy for Management of Unauthorized Disclosures," memorandum, October 2, 2012.

————, "Improving Policy and Procedures for Unauthorized Disclosures Reporting," memorandum, June 19, 2012.

U.S. Code, Title 18, Section 793 (Gathering, transmitting or losing defense information).

————, Title 18, Section 794 (Gathering or delivering defense information to aid foreign government).

————, Title 18, Section 798 (Disclosure of Classified Information).

————, Title 50, Sections 421 et seq. (Protection of Identities of Certain United States Undercover Intelligence Officers, Agents, Informants, and Sources)

USD(I)—*See* Under Secretary of Defense for Intelligence.

U.S. Department of Defense, *Unauthorized Disclosure of Classified Information to the Public*, Directive 5210.50, July 22, 2005.

————, *Clearance of Material for Public Release*, DoD Directive 5230.09, August 22, 2008.

————, *Security and Policy Review of DoD Information for Public Release*, DoD Instruction 5230.29, January 8, 2009.

————, *Counterintelligence Awareness and Reporting (CIAR)*, DoD Directive 5240.06, May 17, 2011a.

————, *DoD Information Security Program and Protection of Sensitive Compartmented Information*, DoD Instruction 5200.01, October 9, 2008, incorporating change of June 13, 2011b.

————, *DoD Information Security Program: Protection of Classified Information, Glossary*, Manual 5200.01-Volume 3, Enclosure 6, February 24, 2012a (as amended).

————, *Countering Espionage, International Terrorism, and the Counterintelligence (CI) Insider Threat*, DoD Directive 5240.26, May 4, 2012b.

————, "Statement from George Little on Defense Initiatives to Limit Unauthorized Disclosures of Classified Information," July 19, 2012c.

————, *Management of the Defense Security Enterprise*, DoD Directive 5200.43, October 1, 2012d.

U.S. Department of Defense Unauthorized Disclosures Working Group, "Strategic Plan," June 1, 2012.

U.S. Secretary of Defense, "Deterring and Preventing Unauthorized Disclosures of Classified Information, memorandum, October 18, 2012.

U.S. White House, *Safeguarding National Security Information*, National Security Decision Directive (NSDD)-84, March 11, 1983.

————, *Classified National Security Information*, Executive Order 13526, December 29, 2009.

————, *Structural Reforms to Improve Security of Classified Networks and the Responsible Sharing of Classified Information*, Executive Order 13587, October 7, 2011.

————, *Protecting Whistleblowers with Access to Classified Information*, Presidential Policy Directive (PPD)-19, October 10, 2012.